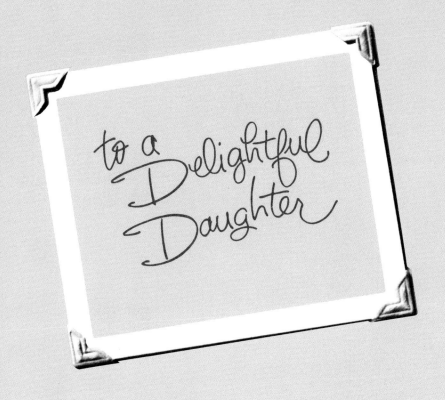

to a Delightful Daughter

The C. R. Gibson Company, Norwalk, Connecticut

Oh, my son's my son till he gets him a wife,
But my daughter's my daughter all her life.

memories

DAUGHTERS ARE DELIGHTFUL!

They arrive in this world all cuddly, soft, full of smiles and seemingly helpless . . . although soon you realize from thrashing arms and healthy screams that these young ladies have minds of their own! But it's too late, the first of many delights has been shown you . . . and you find yourself held captive by the spell of their love.

As little girls, daughters are charmers with fists full of scraggly dandelions and lop-sided grins on mud splattered faces. Moving you to laughter or to tears, they tumble and giggle through the days, then drift off to sleep with a lumpy teddy bear squashed in their arms.

And as toys and dolls are replaced by make-up and perfume, different delights appear — quiet talks about that one special guy, shopping sprees for the perfect dress for the party, and the excitement of that very first date. A daughter's growing-up years have their ups and downs, but you know that everything will turn out O.K. when she throws her arms around you and whispers those enchanting words, "I love you."

Gradually, as days blend into weeks and months into years, a sleek, glowing woman appears before your eyes. You hold her close now, for soon it will be time to let her go. Confidently, a daughter moves to a future full of promise and joy. And you smile with her, for whatever a daughter does, she is always delightful!

A DAUGHTER'S WORLD

For her the sun comes up natural and clear,
As simple light, not source of month and minute;
She takes as wise and proper warmth and year.
This is her world and we live briefly in it.
She holds space in her hands and eyes with ease.
Time is that instant when the night turns real.
Deep in her head are small philosophies
Of want, dislike of don't, and like of feel.

She does not think how other worlds would be.
This way of earth is definite and good.
New day is not a ripe eternity
For her to taste with unbelieving tongue,
But one more chance to walk beyond the wood
And touch the same low grass where birds had sung.

Paul Engle

TO A DAUGHTER

You are the trip I did not take.
You are the pearls I cannot buy.
You are my blue Italian lake.
You are my piece of foreign sky.

Anne Campbell

"WHAT I WANT FOR MY DAUGHTER..."

I ask a twenty-seven-year-old neighbor what it is he wants for his three-year-old daughter, Laurie. He has no glib answer. The question is a huge one, and his answer comes slowly.

"I guess I want her to value herself and know how much she has been loved," this father said. "I want her to be free and strong and know her value and leave us when she should."

It seemed a simple, splendid hope; perhaps no daughter could ask for more.

Gloria Emerson

"Daddy, what were you like when you were little?" How many fathers have heard that question before? And how many have answered with a story, "Once when I was a little kid, just your age . . ."

This is a constant story that I keep telling my daughter who is four years old. She gets something from it and wants to hear it again and again.

When it's time for her to go to bed, she says, "Daddy, tell me about when you were a kid and climbed inside that rock."

"OK."

She cuddles the covers about her as if they were controllable clouds and puts her thumb in her mouth and looks at me with listening blue eyes.

"Once when I was a little kid, just your age, my mother and father took me on a picnic to Mount Rainier. We drove up there in an old car and saw a deer standing in the middle of the road.

"We came to a meadow where there was snow in the shadows of the trees and snow in the places where the sun didn't shine.

"There were wild flowers growing in the meadow and they looked beautiful. In the middle of the meadow there was a huge round rock and Daddy walked over to the rock and found a hole in the center of it and looked inside. The rock was hollow like a small room.

"Daddy crawled inside the rock and sat there staring out at the blue sky and the wild flowers. Daddy really liked that rock and pretended that it was a house and he played inside the rock all afternoon.

"He got some smaller rocks and took them inside the big rock. He pretended that the smaller rocks were a stove and furniture and things and he cooked a meal, using wild flowers for food."

That's the end of the story.

Then she looks up at me with her deep blue eyes and sees me as a child playing inside a rock, pretending that wild flowers are hamburgers and cooking them on a small stove-like rock.

She can never get enough of this story. She has heard it thirty or forty times and always wants to hear it again.

It's very important to her.

I think she uses this story as a kind of Christopher Columbus door to the discovery of her father when he was a child and her contemporary.

Richard Brautigan

FILL A BOWL
WITH MARIGOLDS

Fill a bowl with marigolds
Fill a cup with wine
Capture savage animals
For furs that darkly shine

Fill a plate with succulents
Fill a vault with gold
Fill a chest with finery
All that it can hold

But they shall pass, so better yet
Fill your soul with trust
Fill your heart with laughter
All else is but dust

Fill your eyes with beauty
Fill your heart with prayer
They alone shall last; the rest
Will vanish in the air.

Steve Allen

BALLADE OF LOST OBJECTS

Where are the ribbons I tie my hair with?
      Where is my lipstick? Where are my hose —
The sheer ones hoarded these weeks to wear with
      Frocks the closets do not disclose?
Perfumes, petticoats, sports chapeaux,
      The blouse Parisian, the earring Spanish —
Everything suddenly ups and goes.
      And where in the world did the children vanish?

This is the house I used to share with
      Girls in pinafores, shier than does.
I can recall how they climbed my stair with
      Gales of giggles, on their toptoes.
Last seen wearing both braids and bows
      (But looking rather Raggedy-Annish),
When they departed nobody knows —
      Where in the world did the children vanish?

Two tall strangers, now I must bear with,
　　Decked in my personal furbelows,
Raiding the larder, rending the air with
　　Gossip and terrible radios.
Neither my friends nor quite my foes,
　　Alien, beautiful, stern, and clannish,
Here they dwell, while the wonder grows:
　　Where in the world did the children vanish?

Prince, I warn you, under the rose,
　　Time is the thief you cannot banish.
These are my daughters, I suppose.
　　But where in the world did the children vanish?

Phyllis McGinley

HINTS FOR TEENS

Instructions for teen-agers:

      1. Always leave the shoes in the center of the living-room floor where the parents will be certain to notice them. Let the parents call you three times to come pick up the shoes before you hear them. Then say, "Were you calling *me?*"

      After a few months the parents will pick up the shoes themselves, reasoning that this is easier than shouting your name four times. Once the parent is conditioned to picking up the shoes without making a scene, he will naturally take on other housekeeping chores connected with your presence and cease harassing you to pick up skirts left under your bed, soda pop bottles left in the shower stall, bicycle chains left on the refrigerator, etc.

2. Use the record player at all times while in the house. Acquire no more than six records and play them at peak volume, starting immediately after entering the house and leaving the shoes in the living room.

In a short while the parents will stop saying, "No!" when you ask permission to go out. If dealing with unusually obdurate parents, have three or four friends drop by and bring their records just before the hour when the parents normally sit down to watch Lawrence Welk or to read "The Decline and Fall of the Roman Empire."

3. Arrange to have fifteen or twenty friends telephone you at five-minute intervals at all times while you are out of the house. The parents will eventually tire of answering the phone and come to realize that the phone belongs to you. Thereafter they will be apologetic about asking to use the phone when you are using it to play your record collection to your best friend.

4. When ordered to bathe, always take the best towels. Do not bathe too thoroughly, but merely wet the body enough to produce muddy rivulets in its creases. Use the

best towels to remove the streaks. Then splash water over the bathroom floor and mop it with the towels. Throw the towels under your bed. In due time, the parents will become less insistent about forcing you to bathe when you would prefer to listen to the top forty.

5. Never hide the cigarettes in the kind of places parents use to hide things. You will know from experience what places these are.

6. When using the parents' car, never practice a racing getaway until you are two blocks from the house.

7. After using the parent's necktie or hosiery, remove it and leave it in the dog's or the cat's favorite sleeping place. This will assure you a fashionable wardrobe turnover to keep you in the style forefront of your group.

8. When in need of money, be helpful around the house. Insist upon making breakfast, taking pains to burn the bacon and overcook the coffee. Go off without fanfare and clean your room, being certain to splash the floor wax over the bedspread. When the parents tax you with incom-petence, assume an expression of contrite misery while explaining that they have never given you the opportunity to assume the responsibility of being self-reliant.

If they obtusely miss the point and withhold the money, make the parents feel guilty by reminding them that it was their generation that produced the atomic bomb.

9. Invent another set of parents. Attribute them to Joe or Angela. When the parents are intolerable, tell them things such as, "Angela's parents are letting *her* stay out until midnight," and "Gosh, Joe's parents don't care if *he* has a beer once in a while."

In all cases, the invented set of parents must be shown to have the teen-age spirit. At dinner, for example, it is effective to say, "Gee, Angela's parents listen to the Beatles all day long!" Being compared to Angela's parents will even-tually make other parents feel very old and broken in spirit.

In this condition, it is a small task to reduce them to complete surrender.

Russell Baker

REMEMBRANCE OF
THINGS TO COME

What am I doing, daughter mine?
A-haying while the sun doth shine;
Gathering rosebuds while I may
To hoard against a barren day;
Reveling in the brief sensation
Of basking in your admiration.
Oh, now, when you are almost five
I am the lordliest man alive;
Your gaze is blind to any flaw,
And brimming with respect and awe.
You think me handsome, strong and brave,
You come at morn to watch me shave.
The neighbors' insults lose their sting
When you encourage me to sing,
And like a fashion plate I pose
While you compliment my clothes.
Who wishes his self-esteem to thrive
Should belong to a girl of almost five.
But almost five can't last forever,

And wide-eyed girls grow tall and clever.
Few creatures others less admire
Than a lass of seventeen her sire.
What humiliation must you weather
When we are seen in public together!
Perchance I'll munch a stick of gum,
Or in the theater brazenly hum;
My hat, I'm sure, will flout the law
Laid down for hats at Old Nassau;
My anecdotes you'll strive to stanch,
And at my table manners blanch;
My every word and every deed
Will agony and embarrassment breed;
Your goals of goals, the end of your ends,
To hide me forever from your friends.
Therefore I now chant roundelays,
And rollick in your pride and praise;
Too soon the nymph that you will be
Will shudder when she looks at me.

Ogden Nash

THE LITTLE GIRL AND THE WOLF

One afternoon a big wolf waited in a dark forest for a little girl to come along carrying a basket of food to her grandmother. Finally a little girl did come along and she was carrying a basket of food. "Are you carrying that basket to your grandmother?" asked the wolf. The little girl said yes, she was. So the wolf asked her where her grandmother lived and the little girl told him and he disappeared into the wood.

When the little girl opened the door of her grandmother's house she saw that there was somebody in bed with a nightcap and nightgown on. She had approached no nearer than twenty-five feet from the bed when she saw that it was not her grandmother but the wolf, for even in a nightcap a wolf does not look any more like your grandmother than the Metro-Goldwyn lion looks like Calvin Coolidge. So the little girl took an automatic out of her basket and shot the wolf dead.

Moral: It is not so easy to fool little girls nowadays as it used to be.

James Thurber

BARBIE AND KEN

The real lifesaver of the economy was a pair of teenage dolls who appeared ironically one Christmas stacked (excuse the expression) among the baby dolls who burped, ate, cried, wet, walked, and were as sexless as a stick of gum.

My daughter picked Barbie up off the counter and exclaimed, "Look, Mommy, here is a doll that looks just like you."

I checked out the two-and-a-half-inch bust, the three-inch hips, and the legs that looked like two filter tips without tobacco and said, "She looks like she just whipped through puberty in fifteen minutes."

"I want her," my daughter whined.

Barbie cost $5.98 in the buff, so we purchased a little dress, a pair of pumps, a bra, and a pair of briefs that came to $6.95.

"Aren't we going to buy her a girdle?" asked my daughter.

"Let's wait until she eats and see if she needs one," I said.

If any of us believed for a moment that Barbie was going to be happy as a simple housewife, we were in for a surprise. Barbie was a swinger and she needed the wardrobe to do it.

Within a week, she had three lounge outfits ($5.95 each), an entire pool ensemble ($4.95), two formals ($7.95 each), a traveling suit ($6.95), and skating outfit ($5.00).

One afternoon as I was on my hands and knees fishing Barbie's beach ball out of the sweeper bag, my daughter announced, "Barbie's lonely."

"Terrific!" I said. "Why don't you mail her to Camp Pendleton. And send her satin sheets with her."

"I think we ought to buy Ken."

There was something weird about Ken, but I couldn't put my finger on it. He was a taller version of Barbie who came wearing a jock strap and an insincere smile. He cost $5.98. Within a week, his wardrobe consisted of tennis attire ($7.95), jump suit ($4.95), white tuxedo ($10.95), and a terry cloth robe ($3.95), plus a cardboard car ($12.95). As I explained to my husband, "You don't expect them to sit around night after night passing a beach ball back and forth, do you?"

The little freaks were draining our budget, but I bought some of the patterns and was able to satisfy their clothing appetite by sitting at the sewing machine day and night.

Then one day my daughter announced, "Ken and Barbie are getting married."

It seemed reasonable. After all, they were thrown together day after day in a shoe box under the bed and they were only human.

"What exactly does this mean to me?" I asked.

"Barbie has to have a wedding dress ($10.95) and a trousseau ($36.50) and Ken has to have a tuxedo."

"What's wrong with his white one?" I asked.

"That's for dancing — not marrying," she said.

"Anything else?"

"A wedding party."

"A what!"

"We have to buy Midge and some more people so they'll have people at their wedding."

"Can't you invite some of your other dolls?"

"Would you want someone at your wedding with bowed legs and diapers?"

The wedding was the social event of the year. Our gift to them was a cardboard house that looked like the Hilton.

It was months before all the bills were in but I figured the worst was over. Some families on the block were just starting with their first doll. All that was behind us now.

Then one afternoon in the kitchen, my daughter said excitedly, "Guess what? Barbie's going to have a baby. You're going to be a grandmother."

My eyes welled with self-pity as I ticked off the needs — one naked doctor (who played golf on Wednesdays), two naked nurses (who snorkeled on week-ends), one ambulance driver in the buff who skied, an unclothed intern who . . .

Erma Bombeck

A typical doting father discusses
some of his daughter's charms.

Carol had a charming habit of saying "Hi" every
time she saw you in the house, even if she had so greeted you
in another room five minutes before. You could not run into
her often enough. What else? She said "You're welcome"
to the grocer when, having counted out your change after a
purchase, he said "Thank you." She universalized other
courtesies in which she had been instructed, such as not
pointing in public. She once accused me of not practicing
what I preached when I indicated some artistically disposed
gourds and maple leaves in the autumn window of Mr.
Hawley's dry goods store; I thought better of explaining that
the amenity was not intended to include natural or inanimate
objects, but only people. It is amazing how much parental
love is embodied in laughter at the object. Carol's mother and
I had to leave the room on the occasion of her fourth-birthday
party when we saw her lean toward a celebrant in a dress
with a colossal bow behind and say, "If you're going to be
sick, may I have your orange slices?"

Peter DeVries

LETTER TO MY DAUGHTER
AT THE END OF HER SECOND YEAR

Now it is only hours before you wake
to your third year and to the gifts that lie
piled on the coffee-table, yet I keep
the only gift that it is mine to make.

But how can I offer, among the paper hats,
among the balloons and coloring books and dolls
gleaming with golden hair and the sweet primaries,
this shabby vision of myself seeking,
among these gestures and images, myself?
My gift is wrought, not in the fire of love,
but in the consuming egotism of night
that blots out daughter, lover, wife and friend,
a time to take, my darling, not to give.

So smear this book with the sweetness of your fingers,
and mock with your eyes the brightness of this doll;
come learn our urgent language and put on
mask after mask to match our smiling faces,
seeking what gestures and images may serve
to charm the tall world down from which we smile.

Standing there in the shadow of our gifts,
may you forgive the love that lugged them home,
then turn and take the gift I could not give —
the language of childhood looking for itself
under a mountain of masks and dolls — the poem.

Donald Finkel

NANCY

You are a rose, but set with sharpest spine;
You are a pretty bird that pecks at me;
You are a little squirrel on a tree,
Pelting me with the prickly fruit of the pine;
A diamond, torn from a crystal mine,
Not like that milky treasure of the sea,
A smooth, translucent pearl, but skillfully
Carved to cut, and faceted to shine.

If you are flame, it dances and burns blue;
If you are light, it pierces like a star
Intenser than a needlepoint of ice.
The dexterous touch that shaped the soul of you,
Mingled, to mix, and make you what you are,
Magic between the sugar and the spice.

Elinor Wylie

CONVERSATION WITH MYSELF

This face in the mirror
stares at me
demanding Who are you? What will you become?
and taunting, You don't even know.
Chastened, I cringe and agree
and then
because I'm still young,
I stick out my tongue.

Eve Merriam

BICYCLE RIDER
(to Mary)

Teeth bare to the wind
Knuckle white grip on handle bars
You push the pedals of no return,
Let loose new motion and speed.
The earth turns with the multiplied
Force of your wheels.
Do not look back.
Feet light on the brake
Ride the bicycle of your will
Down the spine of the world,
Ahead of your time, into life.
I will not say —
Go slow.

Eugene McCarthy

TO MY DAUGHTER

Bright clasp of her whole hand around my finger,
My daughter, as we walk together now,
All my life I'll feel a ring invisibly
Circle this bone with shining: when she is grown
Far from today as her eyes are far already.

Stephen Spender

Perhaps the surest way to tell
when a female goes over the boundary
from childhood into meaningful adoles-
cence is to watch how long it takes her
to get to bed at night.

Hildegarde Dolson

THE ROSE FAMILY

The rose is a rose,
And was always a rose.
But the theory now goes
That the apple's a rose,
And the pear is, and so's
The plum, I suppose.
The dear only knows
What will next prove a rose.
You, of course, are a rose —
But were always a rose.

Robert Frost

TO A DEAR DAUGHTER: THE GIFT OF LIGHT

For you, the gentle lights of love,
the knowing someone cares,
with windowed lamps to welcome you,
a nightlight on the stairs.
For you, a fire on the hearth
and warmth of candlelight;
For you, a star left twinkling
to guide you through the night.
For you, a yellow daisy,
reflection from the sun;
A golden dawn to wake you,
the glow of sharing fun.
And ribbons from the rainbow
to hold you in their arc,
because the specialness that's you
will always light the dark.

Virginia Covey Boswell

ACKNOWLEDGMENTS

The editor and the publisher have made every effort to trace the ownership of all copyrighted material and to secure permission from copyright holders of such material. In the event of any question arising as to the use of any material the publisher and editor, while expressing regret for inadvertent error, will be pleased to make the necessary corrections in future printings. Thanks are due to the following authors, publishers, publications and agents for permission to use the material indicated.

STEVE ALLEN, for "Fill A Bowl With Marigolds" from *Wry On The Rocks* by Steve Allen. Copyright © 1956 by Steve Allen.

ATHENEUM PUBLISHERS, INC., for "Letter To My Daughter At The End Of Her Second Year" from *Simeon* by Donald Finkel. Copyright © 1964 by Donald Finkel; for "Conversation With Myself" from *It Doesn't Always Have To Rhyme* by Eve Merriam. Copyright © 1964 by Eve Merriam.

THE DIAL PRESS, for "Sonnet LIII" and "Sonnet LXXV" from *American Child* by Paul Engle. Copyright © 1945, 1956 by Paul Engle, copyright © 1945, 1955 by the Curtis Publishing Company.

DOUBLEDAY & COMPANY, INC., for "Bicycle Rider (to Mary)" from *Other Things And The Aardvark* by Eugene McCarthy. Copyright © 1968 by Eugene McCarthy.

GLORIA EMERSON, for an excerpt from "Your Father's Daughter" by Gloria Emerson. Copyright © 1977 by The Condé Nast Publications, Inc.

HOLT, RINEHART AND WINSTON, for "The Rose Family" from *The Poetry Of Robert Frost* edited by Edward Connery Lathem. Copyright © 1928, 1969 by Holt, Rinehart and Winston, copyright © 1956 by Robert Frost.

ALFRED A. KNOPF, INC., for "Nancy" from *Collected Poems Of Elinor Wylie*. Copyright © 1921 by Alfred A. Knopf, Inc., copyright © renewed 1949 by William Rose Benet.

Selected by Gloria Stashower
Designed by Adair Wilson
Set in Kenntonian Roman and
Kenntonian Italic

PHOTO CREDITS
Doug Mulaire - cover; Jerry Koontz - p. 2; Adair Wilson - p. 6;
James Patrick - p. 11; Bruce Ando - p. 15, 18; Peter Haynes - p. 19, 38;
Gail Russell - p. 21, 35; Cynthia Mergard - p. 24; Jeff Munk; - p. 26;
Robert Wilson - p. 31, Dennis Bradbury - p. 33; Orville Andrews - p. 37;
Ken Blumberg - p. 43.